# What's So Good about Grief, Anyway?

Angela Hamblen, LCSW

*Angela Hamblen*

Copyright © 2013
Angela Hamblen, the Kemmons Wilson Family Center for Good Grief
and Baptist Trinity Hospice

All rights reserved.

An Ellen Rolfes Book

Kemmons Wilson Family Center For Good Grief
1520 W Poplar Ave.
Collierville, TN 38017
(901) 861-5656

ISBN 978-0-9897887-0-0

## IN APPRECIATION

The Kemmons Wilson Family Center for Good Grief gratefully acknowledges its appreciation to the following individuals and organizations that have underwritten the publishing of this children's book. Without their generosity, it would have been impossible to fulfill the dream of WHAT'S SO GOOD ABOUT GRIEF, ANYWAY? and tell the story about our bereavement services.

### The Junior League of Memphis, Inc.

Elaine Childs in memory of her husband, Clarence Childs

Marianne Parrs in memory of her husband, Walter Parrs, Jr.

Sharon Wheeler in memory of her husband, Douglas Wheeler

Anne Wesberry in memory of her husband, Dr. Fred Wesberry

Dr. and Mrs. John Whittemore in memory of Ryan Phillips

### In memory of Selene Jones Benitone

Jeanne & Bill Arthur; Shelley & Coors Arthur; Lyn & Ted Bailey; Danielle & Gray Bartlett; Trevor, Banks and Ella Benitone; Denise Browder; Ginny & Berkeley Burbank; Diane & James Burnett; Jan & Terry Callaway; Jason, Kimberly, Coleman, Connor & Carson Callaway; Amy & Rob Carson; Joyce & Robert Cochran; Cindy and Edward Dobbs; Tenley E. Everette; Meredith & Jason Fair; Kirby & Glenn Floyd; Kimberly & John Freeman; Kathryn & Jim Gilliland; Ginger & Tony Graves; Jackie Gray & Rich Davis; Polly & Steve Havard; Dianne & TW Jones; Elizabeth & Worth Jones; Janis Cox Jones; Lisa Post Lawhead; Janie & Michael Lowery; The Lukken Family: Dana, Walter, William, Genevieve & Crawford; Emily & Jeff McEvoy; The Mershon Family; Kay & Frank Martinez; Abbay & Warren Milnor; Scott & Porter Montgomery; Christy & Ralph Muller; Susan & Joel Myers; Debra, Sara Frances & Josh Neal; Mary Lu & Dave Neuhaus; Amy & Josh Poag; Lauren & Will Plyler; Karen & Murray Riss; Ashley & Bert Robinson; Ellen Rolfes; Alice Goodman Ruthven; Judye & Jack Shannon; Family of Ava Shumake; Lynn Chandler Smith; Leigh Ann, Chris & Elijah Teague; Denese F. Uebelacker & R. Bradford Uebelacker; Haley Uebelacker; Donna & Jon Vanhoozer; Julie & Tal Vickers; Jennifer & Ward Walthal; Barbara & Lewis Williamson

This book is dedicated to several important people.

First, the Camp Good Grief campers. Your courage to confront your sorrow is inspiring.
Thank you for allowing me to walk a part of your grief journey with you.
I cherish my time with you.

Secondly, the Camp Good Grief staff & volunteers. I am so lucky to also call you friends. You are the most giving group of individuals that I have ever met. I will never be able to fully thank you for all you have done for our campers. Just know that your smiles, hugs, high-fives, and encouraging words have changed lives. You are all HEROES to me. I would like to especially thank the Junior League of Memphis for sponsoring Camp Good Grief and for encouraging so many wonderful women to volunteer with us.

Lastly, my father, Paul W. Hamblen, Sr.
Dad, you taught me to do the right thing and to never give up.
You are missed every day.

Angela Hamblen, LCSW

1

Today started off like any other day. Mom had to tell me five times to get up. Dad and my brother, Max, were making cinnamon rolls for breakfast. Our dog, Rascal, was barking and chasing Maggie our cat. Mom started reviewing my spelling words with me while I was trying to eat breakfast. I really do not like spelling and I really do not like spelling tests.
Then Dad yelled out, "OK, the train is leaving in two minutes. Max and Emma, move it!" I am not a morning person and they all know it, but Dad loves to tease me. He started singing,
"Emma, Emma is very slow, but she always makes sure she's wearing her favorite bow."
I yelled, "Dad, stop! Your silly song doesn't even make sense, because I don't wear bows!"
Dad just laughed and said, "Come on my princess, let's get to school."

School started off normal too. Ms. Thomas let us do a fun lab experiment in science. And, we played kickball in gym. We were just about to take our spelling test when Mr. Spencer called me to the office. I was worried I was in trouble, but I was so happy to be missing the spelling test.

When I got to the office, I saw my Aunt Sydney and Max. Aunt Sydney said that she came to take us home. I was super excited because I didn't have to take my spelling test! Woo hoo!!

When we got home, Mom came out and hugged us. Now I was confused. I was wondering why Mom was home. Mom took us inside and said that we needed to talk. We sat down in the living room, which was strange — because we NEVER sit in there. Mom looked at me and her eyes filled with tears. I immediately felt sick to my stomach. I felt like butterflies were in there flying around.

Then she said it -
the worst thing I have ever heard in
my life. She said that my dad died.
I immediately thought — What? When?
My dad is NOT dead! He was just
singing a silly song to me this morning.
NO!! But, I couldn't say anything.
I just cried.
Mom said that Dad had a heart attack
at work and that he died immediately.
Max stormed off and went in his room
and slammed his door. Mom held me and
we both cried. Then I asked if I could
go outside to play basketball.

I couldn't really focus on basketball. I couldn't even make a single basket.
My arms felt like wet noodles. I went and sat down with Rascal.
Rascal just sat with me and licked my face when I cried.

We had so many visitors over the next few days.
A lot of people came over and hugged me. A lot of people cried too.
I'm tired of all of this crying. I want all of this to stop!
I want my dad back and for all of these people to go home!

Dad's funeral was very sweet. My entire class came and my principal came too! I made Dad a card and put it in his casket with him.

Since Dad's funeral, I have had a hard time sleeping. And, I'm too scared to sleep in my bed. Mom let me sleep with her, but she doesn't seem to sleep much. Max hasn't even been home much. He likes to be with his friends. I hear Mom tell people that she is worried about him. I feel worried about everyone. Everybody seems so sad and nobody talks anymore.

Aunt Sydney picks us up each morning and takes us to school. School seems strange, too. I don't always hear what Ms. Thomas says and sometimes I forget to do my work. Ms. Thomas tries to help me, but sometimes I just can't think about anything but my dad. One day in science class, she was teaching us about plants and I just started crying. I was crying so hard that she had to stop class and send me to the school counselor. I was so embarrassed because everyone was looking at me.

The school counselor told me that she was going to talk to my mom and encourage her to take us to counseling. I said, "No! I don't want to go to counseling. Isn't that just for bad kids?" She told me that I wasn't bad, but that I was grieving and that counseling could help my family and me.

One day after school, Mom, Max and I went to counseling at the Center for Good Grief. I was scared. I had no idea what happened in counseling.
Max was angry at Mom for making him go.
He said that he was fine and that he didn't need to talk to anyone.
But, Mom said, "We are going - no debate".

My counselor's name is Annie. She seems nice. We went into a fun looking room at the grief center and we talked and played a game.

She asked me a lot of questions about school, my hobbies, and my family.

6

She told me that lots of families come to the center because someone in their family died. My eyes teared up, but I tried really, really hard not to cry. She asked me if I had ever heard of the word

# Grief

I said yes, but that I didn't really know what it was.

Annie said that grief is all of the feelings and thoughts that run around inside of us after someone we love dies. I thought, "Well, I must be grieving because it feels like a roller coaster is running around inside of me". She asked me if I would come back and work more with her. I said, "Yes." I think maybe she can really help me.

We went back to the Center for Good Grief every few weeks. I started looking forward to seeing Annie. It got easier to talk to her and to talk about my dad. I told her that I was having a hard time sleeping because I felt scared at night. And, I told her that I had several bad nightmares. I told her that I really wish I knew somebody else whose dad died, because everyone at school has a dad, except for me!

We also talked a lot about Dad.
I told her that my dad always let
me sit in his lap and watch TV.
I told her that my dad kept us safe
because he was a police officer.
I told her that my dad was really
funny and that he would
sometimes dance through the
den and make up songs
about our family.

I really miss his funny dances and songs.
As soon as I said that, I started thinking about the last song he made up
about me and my bow and I started crying. Annie just let me.
She said that crying helps us feel better.
Before I left, I asked Annie if I could sing one of my dad's songs for her.
She said, "Please!" I started singing and dancing like my dad.
All of a sudden we were both laughing! It felt good to laugh again.
Annie said that she thinks I am funny like Dad.
That makes me feel good — to think about being like Dad.

One day when I went to see Annie,
I decided to tell her about the day my dad died.
I told her that he had a heart attack and died.
I told Annie that I didn't believe Mom and that I kept thinking
it was all a bad dream and that Dad would come back.
I told Annie that I sometimes think I hear him,
but then I remember he died.

Annie told me that she is proud of me and how hard I have worked
on my grief and that she wanted me to go to Camp Good Grief.
She told me that camp is a lot of fun and that
it would help me with my grief.
I felt scared to go, but Annie said it would really help me.
I gave in and said, "OK." But, I don't really want to go.
Who would ever want to go to a grief camp?

I woke up with a stomachache today because I have to go to camp – Camp Good Grief.

Imagine that, a camp all about grief! And, they call it good grief!

What's so good about grief, anyway?

I can't think of one good thing! At least Max gets to wait until the fall to go to the Teen Camp Good Grief! I don't get to wait.

Ugh!! I'm feeling very angry! I wish I had told Annie, "No."
I'm angry that I have to go to this camp…angry that my dad died.

Now I'm feeling nervous.
There are so many kids here.
Mom reminds me that
somebody in their lives died too.

I can't imagine that
ALL of these people are grieving.
I wonder if any of
their dads have died.

I finally see Annie. Seeing her makes me feel a little better. She looks different in camp clothes and she's wearing a tiara. She says that she is Queen Annie at camp. I had no idea she could be so silly.

Annie introduces me to my buddy, Janet. All of a sudden, I feel special. I have my very own buddy. I looked around and noticed that every camper has their very own buddy. Janet is really nice. She tells me that we are going to have so much fun at camp. FUN?!?! I think, "It's a grief camp, how can it possibly be fun!" Then I wonder if Janet's dad died. I really want to meet someone else whose dad has died.

Janet says, "Come on Emma, it's time to board the bus." I give my mom a hug and say goodbye. I want to cry, but I don't. I get on the bus with Janet; I know I can't avoid camp anymore.

Well, this sure is confusing! We are going to grief camp and people are smiling, singing and even laughing!!! I feel like I got on the wrong bus!
Sam and Grace are handing out candy to the campers. Bill and Mr. Jake are telling jokes and LaTonya, Bailey and Hannah are singing songs. Everyone seems happy. I don't know what to do. Sometimes at home I feel bad if I'm having fun…you know because Dad can't have fun anymore.
I feel like if I have fun, I am forgetting him.
Oh, I really miss him.

"Welcome to Camp Good Grief," exclaims Queen Annie.
Then she asks, "Who knows what makes Camp Good Grief different from any other camp?"

Oh no, I feel scared and nervous...two strange feelings at the same time.
Queen Annie is going to talk about why we are here.
Talking about my dad makes me cry.
I'm scared to cry in front of people, because
I don't want to look like a baby.

But Ian, another camper, confidently raises his hand and he says, "We are here because somebody we loved died."

Just like that he could
say it out loud.
I think he is brave.
I wonder if his dad died too.
Queen Annie says,
"That's right, we are all here
because someone we loved died."

I feel so sad.
But, as I look around I see a lot of sad kids like me.
Maybe they do feel like me.
Queen Annie tells us that we are going to
work hard on our grief while having lots of fun!

She and the volunteers get everyone
up to sing and play silly games.
It feels funny to be at grief camp
and to be laughing.

Mr. Jake stands up
and yells,
"It's time for
water games!"
Everyone is excited.

Janet says, "Come on, let's go have some fun."
It feels good to run around. Janet is so fun.
She tried to steal water balloons from Mr. Jake and Levi,
but they got her every time.

I surprised Janet and got her wet when she wasn't looking.
I ran and ran; it was so fun.
I was surprised that I was starting
to have fun
at
Camp Good Grief.

After we played water games, it was time for grief group.
I am in Ms. Ruth's group; I think we are the best group! I'm surprised
to see other kids like me talking about their grief.
Jacob and Marcus are at camp because their moms died.
Lillian and Sam are here because their brothers died.
Monica, Bailey and Corey are here because their dads died!!
Can you believe it??? Even three people like me!!!

We all brought pictures of our loved ones to group
so we could talk about them and how they died.
I was feeling nervous and was hiding my picture.
I was afraid to talk about my dad; I was afraid of crying.
But guess what? Other campers cried.

Marcus cried when he talked about his mom and
said that he misses the special grilled cheese
sandwiches she made him.
Sam said that he misses playing video games
with his brother.
He said that he doesn't really like to play them
anymore, because he has to play alone.
Lillian cried and said that sometimes she gets scared at night.
I do too…it made me feel a little better to hear her say that.
Monica and Corey began crying, but Bailey didn't.
Bailey said that she is afraid to cry. All of a sudden I said, "Me too!"
The next thing I knew I was talking about my dad,
and I even showed my very favorite picture of him, the two of us
fishing together in Florida.

I told them that my dad was my hero.
I told them that he was brave and that he was a police officer.
I told them that he always came to my basketball games and
that he always cheered for me.
Then I told them about the terrible, awful day that he died.
I told them all about his heart attack.
Jacob spoke up and said that his mom died from a heart attack.
I couldn't believe that he could understand some of my feelings — like shock.
We both felt shock that they could be here one minute and
then, all of a sudden without warning, they died.
I started feeling a little more normal because it seemed like
I wasn't the only one out there with all of these feelings.
Then Corey said that his dad died suddenly too.
He said it feels like his dad is away on a trip.
Bailey said that she worries about her mom and sister.
I worry about my mom too. Mom cries a lot and
she doesn't like to cook anymore.
My aunt comes over a lot now and she takes me to school and practice.
I wish my dad could take me.

We did so many different activities
that helped me talk about my
feelings and
my special memories
of my dad.

My buddy, Janet, is so much fun.
She acts silly with me,
but she also
listens when I want to talk.
I started feeling relaxed and peaceful.
My grief did not seem so scary anymore.

On the last day of camp, we had a memorial service.
We wrote letters to our loved ones that we attached to yellow balloons.
I felt proud because I worked so hard on my dad's letter.
I even drew him a picture. Dad loved my pictures.
He would always hang them up at work.
In my letter, I wrote:

Dear Dad,
 I miss you every day. I miss your cinnamon rolls - mom always burns them. I miss your silly songs and your dances. I am sorry I got mad at you that morning. I hope you aren't mad at me. I know I am your special princess and I'm trying to make you proud. You were the best dad in the world! I really like it here at camp. I have learned a lot about my feelings. I am feeling better. I am sorry you died. I will always love you. Rascal misses you too!
 Love, Me
 xoxoxo

At the memorial service, I felt sad, mad and happy all at the same time.
I was happy because I knew that my dad loved me so much;
I was his special princess!
But, I was also sad and mad that I can't see him or talk to him anymore.
Queen Annie called us up one at a time to release our balloons.
Jacob went first. Then Marcus, Lillian, Sam, Monica, Bailey and Corey.
I watched them each go. They all worked hard on their letters too.

Then, it was my turn.
I felt confident.
I wasn't afraid to cry anymore.
I learned that it's ok to cry,
and I knew everyone there
understood how I felt.
As I walked up to release my
yellow balloon, I cried and
cried for my dad.
But, I did watch my balloon
float away to heaven.

Janet hugged me and let me cry.
She told me that she was proud of me and that she knew my dad loved me.
After a few minutes, I stopped crying.
I sat there and watched the other campers release their letters
and balloons. I didn't know each camper's story, but I knew that
we all had so much in common.
I knew that we had learned that you have to work on
your grief in order to feel better.
And, I was surprised to realize that I was feeling better.

Then it hit me;
there IS something good about grief.
The good is knowing that you
don't have to grieve by yourself.
The good is in all the memories,
memories that will always be with you.
The good is knowing that talking about
your feelings is what makes you feel better.

The good is knowing you are going to be ok —
you can grieve and have fun!

I feel sad that camp is ending. I wish I could come here every day.
Then, Janet told me that she went to Camp Good Grief when she was 10 after her dad died, and that now she comes to volunteer as a buddy.
I hugged Janet, because I knew that she knew what
I had been feeling all along.
She said that in a few years I would be old enough to volunteer too.
I felt so excited and said,
"Yes, I want to come back and help campers
find the good in their grief!"

I said goodbye to all of my new friends,
including Janet.

I hugged Queen Annie and said,
"I'll see you next week at
my appointment."

I got in the car with Mom and
started telling her all about
camp and everything I learned.

the end

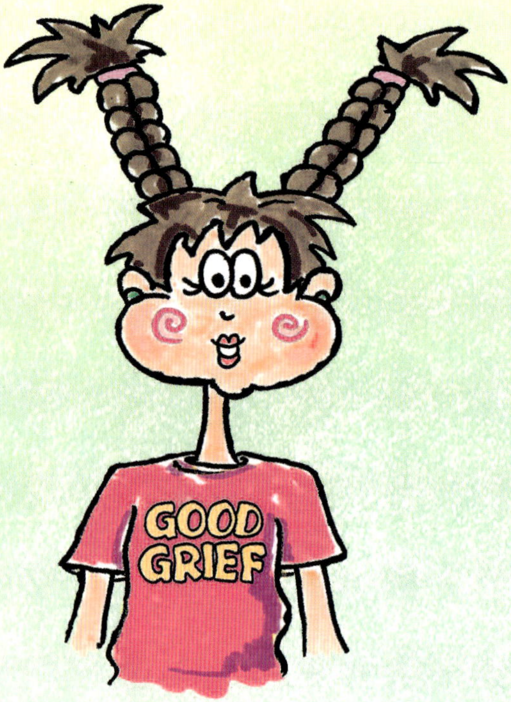
GOOD
GRIEF

## ABOUT THE AUTHOR

Angela Hamblen, L.C.S.W., is the Clinical Director for the Kemmons Wilson Family Center for Good Grief which is a part of Baptist Trinity Hospice, a division of the Baptist Memorial Health Care System serving Tennessee, Arkansas and Mississippi. Angela is a licensed clinical social worker trained specifically in the field of death and dying. She directs the three Camp Good Grief programs offered to children, teens and adults who are grieving the loss of a loved one. After the tragedy of September 11, Angela served as a consultant to Schneider Children's Hospital in Long Island, NY where a program modeled after Camp Good Grief was developed.

She is a recipient of several community awards, including:
Top 40 Under 40, Health Care Hero Finalist, An Angel in Our Midst,
and 50 Women Who Make A Difference.

## ABOUT THE ILLUSTRATOR

Nikki Schroeder, professional artist and graphic designer, began her career when she was still a college student at Memphis State University. In 1987, she opened Graffiti Graphics, a full service graphic design studio in Memphis, TN. With over 26 years experience, she is a leader in the branding industry, providing cutting edge designs and marketing services to successful companies and organizations nationally. Nikki is also the co-founder, co-editor and creator of Jabberblabber Earth Friendly Family Magazine, a monthly publication provided FREE to children in Memphis and the surrounding areas.

She is a recipient of 50 Women Who Make A Difference.

## KEMMONS WILSON FAMILY CENTER FOR GOOD GRIEF

As the first comprehensive and only bereavement center for children, teens and adults in the Mid South region, the Center for Good Grief provides support for individuals who are grieving the death of a loved one. The Center was built by private contributions including a lead capital campaign gift from the family of the late Kemmons Wilson, Sr. As a program of Baptist Trinity Hospice, the Center for Good Grief is appropriately located adjacent to Baptist Trinity Hospice House on the campus of Baptist Memorial Hospital – Collierville, TN.

Our mission is to provide a safe environment, available year round, for children, teens, and adults to explore and express their feelings related to the death of a loved one and learn to thrive in a world without that special person. The Center allows them to share their experience with others as they move through the healing process – all in a therapeutic environment guided by licensed mental health professionals specializing in bereavement.

All our services are free of charge and are made possible through individual donations and grants funded through/by the Baptist Memorial Health Care Foundation, in addition to donations from various organizations and corporations.

Kemmons Wilson Family Center For Good Grief
1520 W Poplar Ave.
Collierville, TN 38017
(901) 861-5656

If you would like to make a tax deductible contribution to the Kemmons Wilson Family Center for Good Grief, please send check payable to:
Baptist Memorial Health Care Foundation, 350 N. Humphreys Blvd., Memphis, TN 38120
and mark for "Center for Good Grief" or call toll free: 800.895.4483.
You can also make a secure on-line donation at www.bmhgiving.org